Contents

Words in **bold** can be found in the glossary on p.30

Sound

We live in a world filled with many different sounds. There are sounds around us all the time. You might think you are in a quiet room, but try shutting your eyes and listening carefully. How many different sounds can you hear?

Some sounds, like shouting, are very loud. Other sounds, like a whisper, are very quiet. Some sounds, like foghorns, are very low. Other sounds, like whistles, are very high.

An aeroplane taking off is noisy. ➡

HOW does Science Work?

Sound

written by
Carol Ballard

WAYLAND

Published in paperback in 2014 by Wayland
Copyright © 2014 Wayland

Hachette Children's Books
338 Euston Road, London NW1 3BH

Commissioning Editor: Vicky Brooker
Editors: Laura Milne, Camilla Lloyd
Senior Design Manager: Rosamund Saunders
Design and artwork: Peta Phipps
Commissioned Photography: Philip Wilkins
Consultant: Dr Peter Burrows
Series Consultant: Sally Hewitt
Artwork p.11: Peter Bull

ISBN: 978 0 7502 8248 2

Printed and bound in China

10 9 8 7 6 5 4 3 2 1

British Library Cataloguing in Publication Data
    Ballard, Carol
    Sound. - (How does science work?)
    1.Sound - Juvenile literature
    I.Title
    534

Wayland is a division of Hachette Children's Books, an
Hachette UK Company.
www.hachette.co.uk

Acknowledgements:

Cover photograph: Drumming on Snare Drum, Louie
Psihoyos/Getty Images

Photo credits: Austin Brown/Getty Images 4, Richard
Price/Getty Images 6, Jonathan Cavendish/Corbis 7, Lothar
Lenz/Corbis 12, Richard Kolker/Getty Images 13, Phillip
Colla/Ecoscene 14, Chris Shinn/Getty Images 16, Conrad
Zobel/Corbis 18, LA/CABYVALENCE/Photolibrary 19, John
Birdsall 20, Lemoine/PhotoLibrary 21, Arne Hodalic/Corbis
22, Merlin Tuttle/Science Photo Library 23, Louie
Psihoyos/Corbis 26.

The author and publisher would like to thank the models
Kodie Briggs, Dylan Chen, Jessica Li Murphy and
Isabelle Li Murphy.

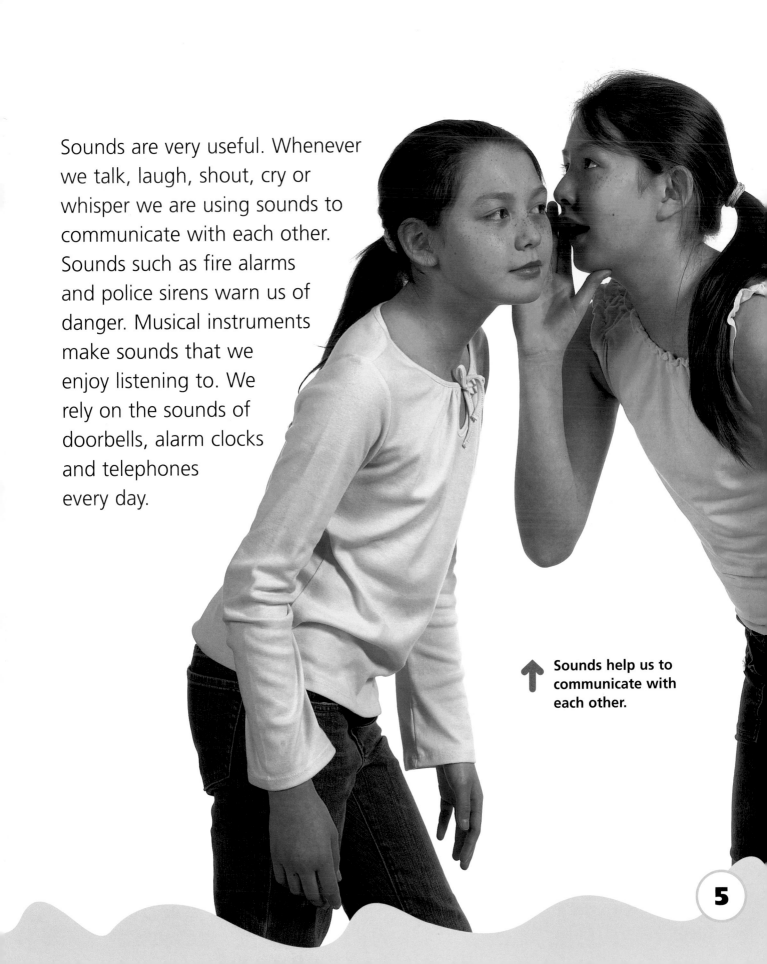

Sounds are very useful. Whenever we talk, laugh, shout, cry or whisper we are using sounds to communicate with each other. Sounds such as fire alarms and police sirens warn us of danger. Musical instruments make sounds that we enjoy listening to. We rely on the sounds of doorbells, alarm clocks and telephones every day.

↑ **Sounds help us to communicate with each other.**

Where does sound come from?

Anything that makes a sound is called a **sound source**. Some sounds are made by the world in which we live. These are **natural** sound sources, such as the clap of thunder in a storm or the rustling of leaves in a breeze.

Waves crashing on rocks are a natural sound source. →

Some sound sources are made by living things. These are **living** sound sources, such as dogs barking or birds singing.

Some sounds come from machines. These are **artificial** or **man-made** sound sources. Radios, alarm bells and electric drills are all artificial sound sources.

Cats make a purring sound when they are stroked.

How does sound travel?

Sound travels away from a sound source in all directions. A sound is made when a sound source **vibrates**. This means that it makes tiny, very fast backwards and forwards movements. As it does so, it makes the air around it vibrate too.

Guitar strings vibrate when they are plucked. →

The vibrations travel through the air, spreading out in wider and wider circles. These vibrations in the air are called **sound waves**.

TRY THIS! Make waves

1   You will need a bowl and some plasticine.

2   Get your bowl and half fill it with water.

3   Drop the small ball of plasticine into the middle.

4   Watch what happens to the surface of the water.

You should find that ripples spread out in wider and wider circles, away from the place where you dropped the plasticine. Sound waves travel through the air in the same way as the ripples travel through the water.

Sound travels at an amazing speed – about 344 metres (1,129 feet) every second through the air!

How do we hear?

We use our ears to hear sounds around us. When you look at your ears in a mirror, you see two flaps, one on each side of your head. These flaps are the outside part of your ear. The rest of each ear is hidden inside your head. Sound waves entering our ears allow us to hear.

← The outside part of your ears are called pinna.

sound messages to the brain

middle ear

sound

pinnae

eardrum

inner ear

outer ear

 A diagram of the ear.

Sound waves travel into the **pinna** and through the outer ear. At the end of the **outer ear** is a thin layer of skin called the **eardrum**. The sound waves make the eardrum vibrate. The vibrations travel through the **middle ear**. Then vibrations travel along a spiral in the **inner ear**. The vibrations then connect to the **nerves** which send messages to the brain. The brain works out what you are hearing.

Why do we have two ears?

Having two ears helps us to pinpoint which direction a sound is coming from. If one ear points towards a sound source, the sound waves will reach it just before they reach the other ear. The brain will get a message from that ear before it gets the message from the other ear. This helps your brain to work out which direction the sound came from.

Many animals can move their ears. This means that they can pinpoint the direction a sound is coming from much more accurately than humans.

Dogs have good hearing because they can move their ears.

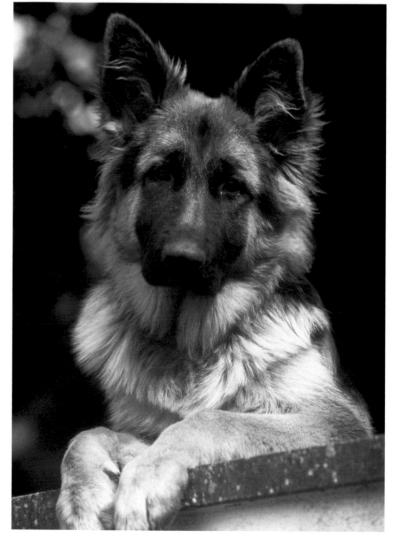

TRY THIS! Pinpoint sounds

1 Cover your eyes with a blindfold or scarf.

2 Ask some friends to clap one by one in different positions around you.

3 See if you can tell which direction the sound is coming from.

4 Try and guess who is closest to you.

You could probably pinpoint the direction of the sounds. Animals such as dogs, have much better hearing and can tell where sounds come from more accurately.

If your eyes are covered and you cannot see where the sound is coming from you can use your ears.

Your ears help you to tell which direction the sound is coming from.

↑ **Can you tell where a sound comes from?**

What can sound travel through?

Sound needs something to travel through. It can travel through air and other gases. It can travel through water and other liquids. Sound can travel through solid materials too. Sound cannot travel through an empty space. There is no sound on the Moon because there is no air for sound to travel through.

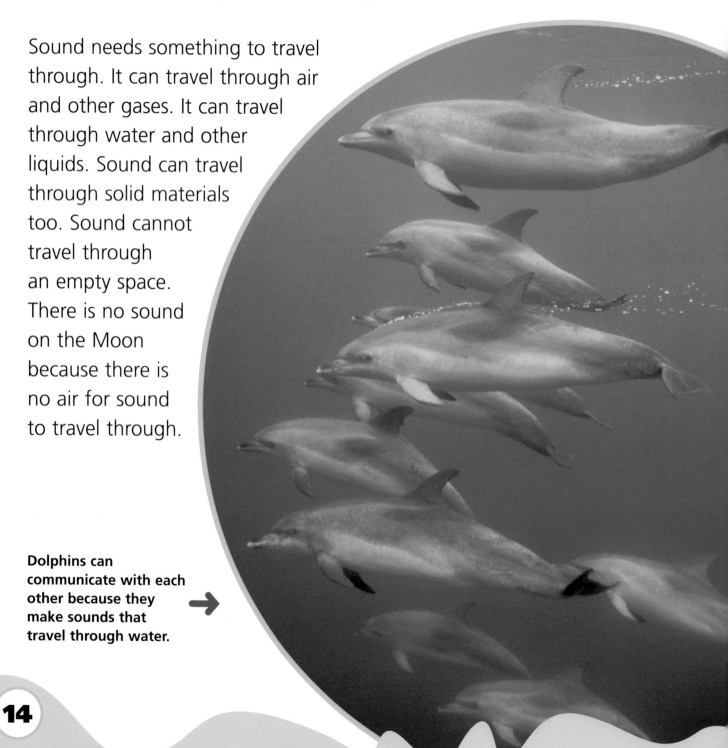

Dolphins can communicate with each other because they make sounds that travel through water. →

TRY THIS! Make a string telephone

1 You will need some scissors, two plastic pots and some string.

2 Make a small hole in the bottom of each of the plastic pots.

3 Thread a length of string through each hole.

4 Tie a knot in each end of the string so that the pots are linked together.

5 Give one pot to a friend. Walk away until the string is tight.

6 Speak into your pot – your friend should hear your voice by holding the pot to their ear.

This is a string telephone. It works because sound travels along the string.

Take care using scissors

↑ **You can use a string telephone to send messages.**

Blocking sounds

Sounds can travel more easily through some materials than others. Sounds can travel through air, liquids and through hard materials like metal or wood.

Sound travels less easily through soft, squashy materials like foam and thick fabrics. Materials that sound cannot travel easily through can be used to block sound. They are called **sound insulators**.

This man works in a very noisy place, so he wears ear protectors to stop his ears being hurt. →

TRY THIS! Block sounds

1 Find some different materials such as sponges, wood and cloth – you will need two pieces of each material.

2 Ask a friend to cover their ears with the first material.

3 Make a sound. How well can your friend hear you?

4 Test each of your materials to see which ones sound travels through easily and which ones sound doesn't travel through as well.

You should find that the softer and thicker the material, the better they are at blocking the sound.

Looking after your ears

Ears are delicate and should be looked after properly so that they work well throughout our lives. Loud noises are especially bad for ears and can cause permanent harm.

Turning the **volume** down on personal stereos, and avoiding using them for long periods, can help your ears. People who work in very noisy places or use noisy machinery should wear ear protectors to prevent damage to their ears.

Pop concerts can be very loud and damage your ears.

Ears need to be kept clean. This reduces the build-up of dirt and the chance of infections. Earache is a common problem and you may need to visit a doctor if your ears hurt. By looking inside the ear with an **otoscope**, the doctor can see what is causing the earache. Medicine can often cure the problem.

Doctors can examine your ears using an instrument called an otoscope.

Being deaf

People who are **deaf** and **hard of hearing** cannot hear properly. They need special ways of coping with everyday life. These people use sign language to communicate.

People who are deaf and hard of hearing cannot hear things such as alarm clocks, fire alarms and television programmes. A flashing light can replace the ringing or alarm sound so deaf people can see them instead. Subtitles of conversations in films and on television help them understand.

 Sign language is a way of talking by using hand gestures.

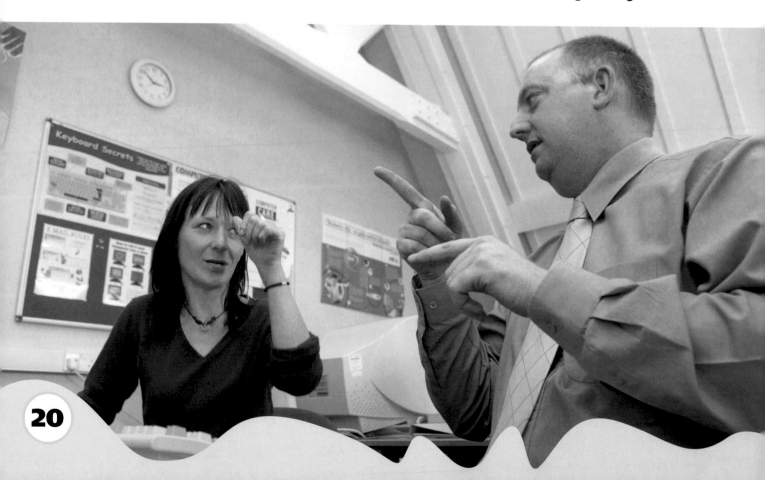

Many deaf and hard of hearing people wear **hearing aids** that make sounds louder and easier to hear.

They can often lip-read. They watch the shapes and movements of a speaker's lips and work out the sounds that are spoken.

Hearing dogs can help too. They are trained to alert their owners when they hear important sounds such as telephones or doorbells.

Hearing aids are tiny microphones that fit inside or behind the ear.

What is an echo?

An **echo** is a sound bouncing back from a long way away. If you shout loudly in a place like a cave, you might hear your voice again several times.

The sound of your voice travels through the cave. When it hits the hard stone of the cave wall, it bounces off. When it reaches your ears, you hear it again. This is an echo.

Caves are common places to hear echoes.

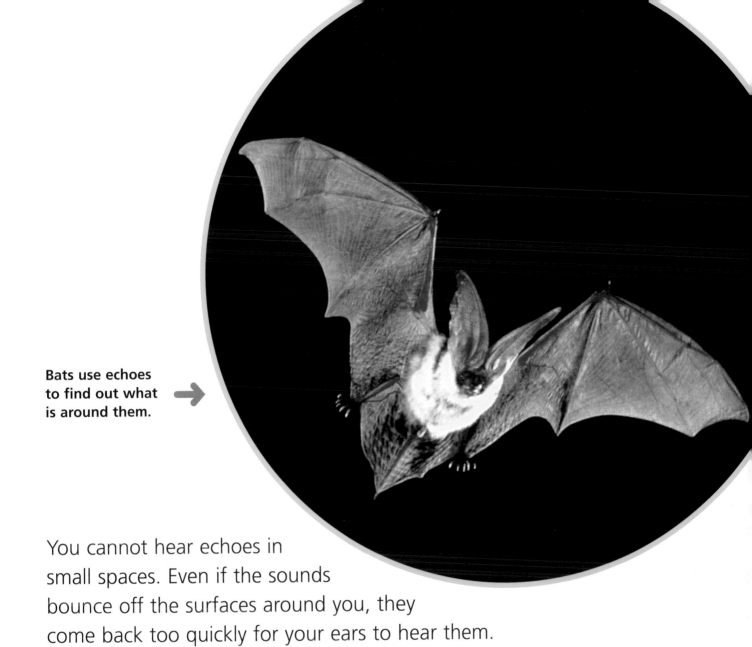

Bats use echoes to find out what is around them.

You cannot hear echoes in small spaces. Even if the sounds bounce off the surfaces around you, they come back too quickly for your ears to hear them.

Some animals use echoes. Bats send out a series of tiny squeaks, which bounce back from things around them. By detecting the echoes, the bats can fly without bumping into things. They are also able to find their **prey** in this way. Whales and dolphins also use echoes to help them find their way.

High or low?

How high or low a sound is, is called its **pitch**. If a pebble is dropped into water, ripples will spread out in all directions. If the ripples are very close together, they will seem to move very fast and there will be a lot of them. If the ripples are further apart, they will seem to move slowly and there will be fewer of them.

Sound waves act in the same way. The differences in the waves make the different pitches of the sound. Fast, close sound waves make high-pitched sounds. Slow, far apart sound waves make low-pitched sounds.

low pitch

Slow, far apart waves make low sounds

high pitch

Fast, close waves make high sounds

TRY THIS! Make different pitches

1 You will need several glass bottles or drinking glasses.

2 Pour different amounts of water into each.

3 Gently tap each glass or bottle with a metal spoon.

4 Try to put your bottles in order of pitch – start with the lowest on the left.

You should find that the more water there is in a bottle, the lower the sound it makes.

This is because the more water there is, the slower the sound waves travel.

Wow!

Elephants can hear sounds that are much too low for humans to hear!

Loud or quiet?

How loud or quiet a sound is, is called its volume. Sound waves can be very big or very small. Different sizes of sound waves make sounds of different volumes. Big sound waves make loud sounds and small sound waves make quiet sounds.

If you bang a drum hard, large sound waves are made.

TRY THIS! Making vibrations

1 You will need some clingfilm, a bowl and some rice.

2 Stretch a piece of clingfilm tightly over the top of a bowl.

3 Put a few grains of rice on top of the clingfilm.

4 Tap the clingfilm gently with one finger. Listen to the sound and watch the rice.

5 Tap the clingfilm harder, and then even harder.

You should find that the harder you tap the clingfilm, the louder the sound. The louder the sound the bigger the vibrations, and so the higher the rice grains will jump.

Measuring sound

The volume of a sound is measured in units called **decibels**. The volume of a sound can be measured using an instrument called a **decibel meter**.

Some sounds are so quiet that humans cannot hear them. The quietest sound we can hear is called the **hearing threshold**, at 0 decibels. When sounds are very loud they are close to the **threshold of pain** and then they can hurt our ears!

This is a decibel scale showing the volumes of sounds.

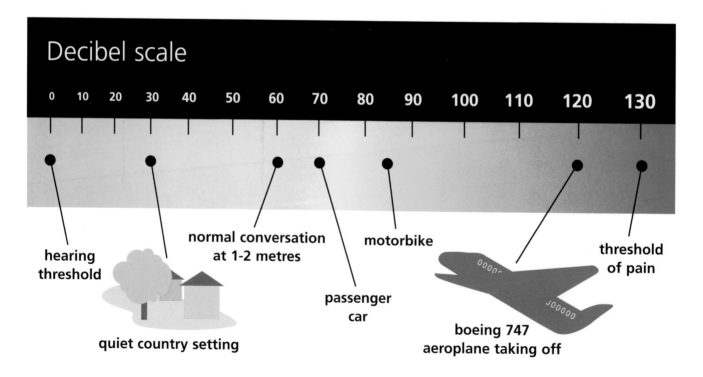

Decibel scale

| 0 | 10 | 20 | 30 | 40 | 50 | 60 | 70 | 80 | 90 | 100 | 110 | 120 | 130 |

hearing threshold

quiet country setting

normal conversation at 1-2 metres

passenger car

motorbike

boeing 747 aeroplane taking off

threshold of pain

Sounds can be a nuisance and disturb people around them. Places that are very noisy can be asked to lower the sound levels. Sounds we do not want to hear are called **noise pollution**.

If you try banging a saucepan with a spoon you will see that you can make a loud sound. This means that the sound waves are large.

Banging a saucepan with a wooden spoon makes a very loud sound. →

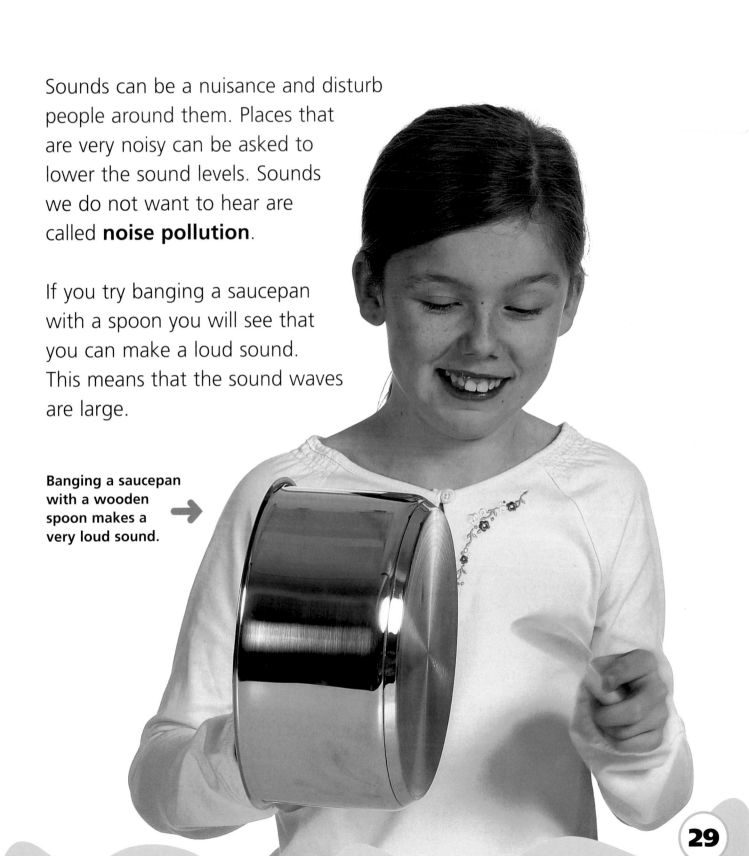

Glossary

artificial made by machinery or equipment

deaf unable to hear properly

decibels units for the volumes of a sound

decibel meter an instrument that measures the volume of a sound

eardrum thin layer of skin inside the ear

echo a sound bouncing back

hard of hearing unable to hear properly

hearing aid device to help deaf people hear

hearing threshold the point where you can hear the quietest sounds

inner ear the part of the ear deep inside the head

living alive

man-made made by people

middle ear part of the ear between outer ear and inner ear

natural to do with the world around us

nerves parts of the body that carry messages

noise pollution unwanted noise

otoscope a medical instrument for examining the ear

outer ear outermost part of the ear

pinna part of the ear you can see at the side of the head

pitch how high or low a sound is

prey animal that is food for another animal

sound insulators materials that block sounds

sound source anything that makes a sound

sound waves vibration that carries a sound

threshold of pain the point where sounds become painful to your ears

vibrates move backwards and forwards rapidly

volume how loud or quiet a sound is

Further information

Books to read

Sound: Listen Up by Wendy Sadler,
Science in your Life series,
Raintree, 2005

Light and Sound by Chris Oxlade,
Wayland, Hachette Children's
Books, 2005

Sound: From Whisper to Rock Band
by Chris Cooper, Science Answers
series, Heinemann Library, 2004

Sound by Rebecca Hunter,
Raintree, 2004

Sound and Hearing, by Claire
Llewellyn, Start-Up Science series,
Evans Brothers, 2004

Websites to visit

**www.bbc.co.uk/education/
dynamo/lab/make.shtml**
Full of experiments you can do
at home.

**www.bbc.co.uk/schools/
scienceclips**
Lots of interesting information and
quizzes to test your knowledge.

CD Roms to explore

*Play and Learn: Science
Experiments,* Dorling
Kindersley, 2000

Become a Science Explorer, Dorling
Kindersley, 2000

Index